PRINT HANDWRITING WORKBOOK

For Kids

THIS BOOK BELONGS TO

....

....

....

TABLE OF CONTENTS

Hey there, Young Writer!
Let's practice, laugh, and learn together!

Chloe Felix, a beloved author, brings joy to children with her engaging books. Her work inspires and ignites children's boundless imaginations and promotes skills development through delightful and educational content, nurturing a love for learning, creativity, and positive values.

Disclaimer:
This handwriting workbook is designed for educational and practice purposes only. While every effort has been made to ensure the accuracy and appropriateness of the content, the publisher and author are not responsible for any errors or omissions.
The exercises, jokes, riddles, affirmations, quotes, facts, and writing prompts in this book are intended to aid handwriting practice and provide entertainment and inspiration. They are not intended as professional advice or to replace guidance from educators or caregivers. Results may vary. Consult educators or healthcare providers for concerns about writing abilities.

TIPS FOR OUTSTANDING HANDWRITING

1. Sit up straight: Good posture helps you write better

2. Hold your pencil right: Not too tight or loose – just right.

3. Take your time: Practice each letter and word slowly and carefully.

4. Practice daily: Even 10 minutes a day makes a big difference.

5. Line it up: Pay attention to where your letters sit on the lines.

6. Start with warm-ups: Wiggle your fingers and stretch your hands before writing.

7. Stay consistent: Try to make your letters the same size.

8. Be patient: Don't rush - take your time with each letter.

9. Be proud: Celebrate every improvement, no matter how small!

BEFORE AND AFTER

On the first day you use this book, write the sentence below in your current handwriting.
After you finish the book, write the same sentence again and celebrate your improvement!

....

Sentence to write:
Challenges make me stronger and smarter.

....

Before Practice   Date:..........................

_____

_____

_____

_____

_____

_____

_____

_____

_____

After Practice   Date:..........................

_____

_____

_____

_____

_____

_____

_____

_____

_____

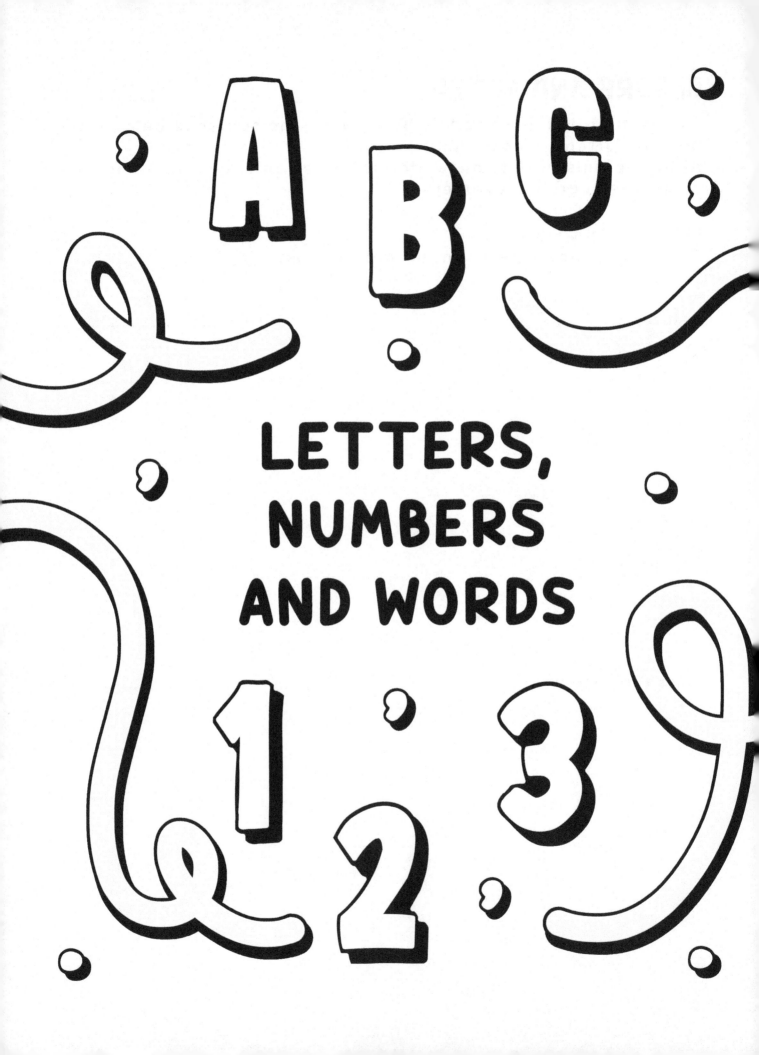

LETTERS, NUMBERS AND WORDS

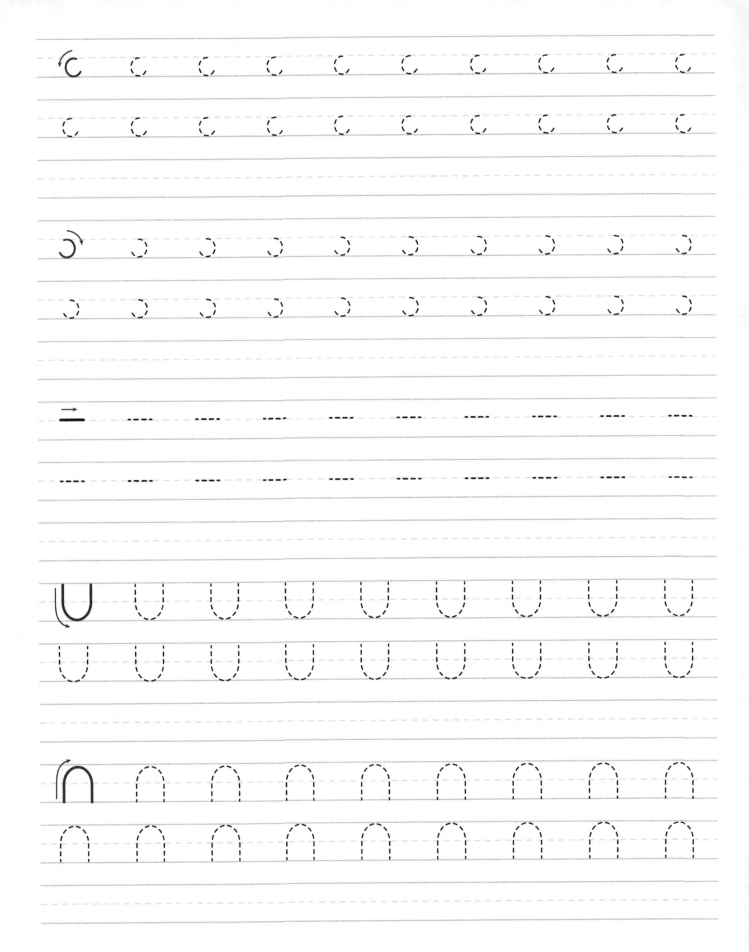

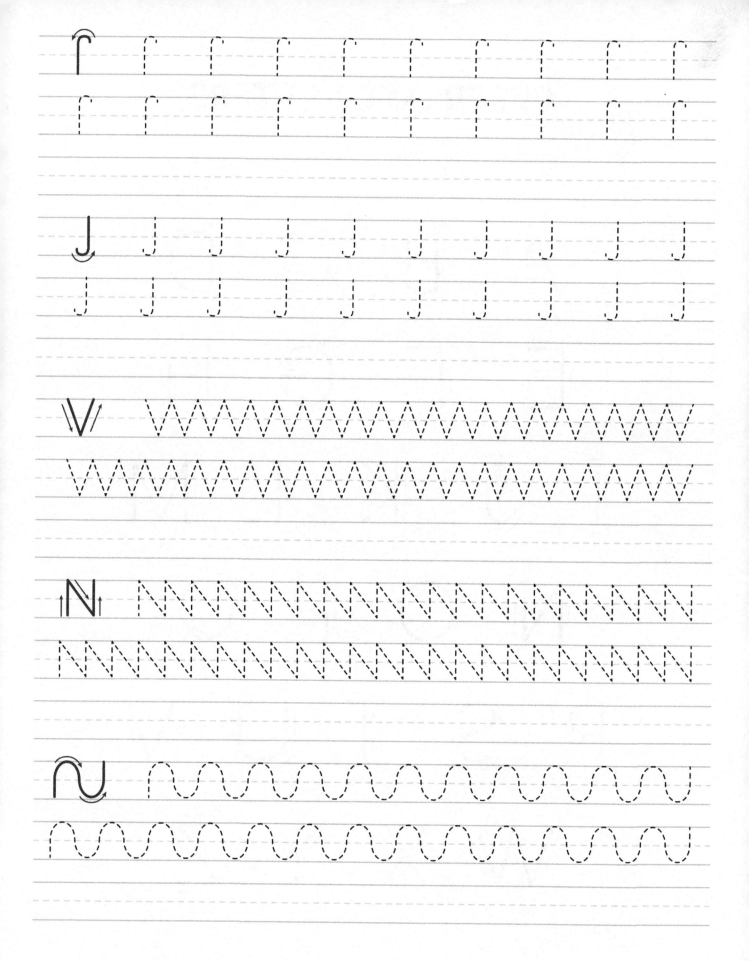

LOWERCASE LETTERS AND NUMBERS

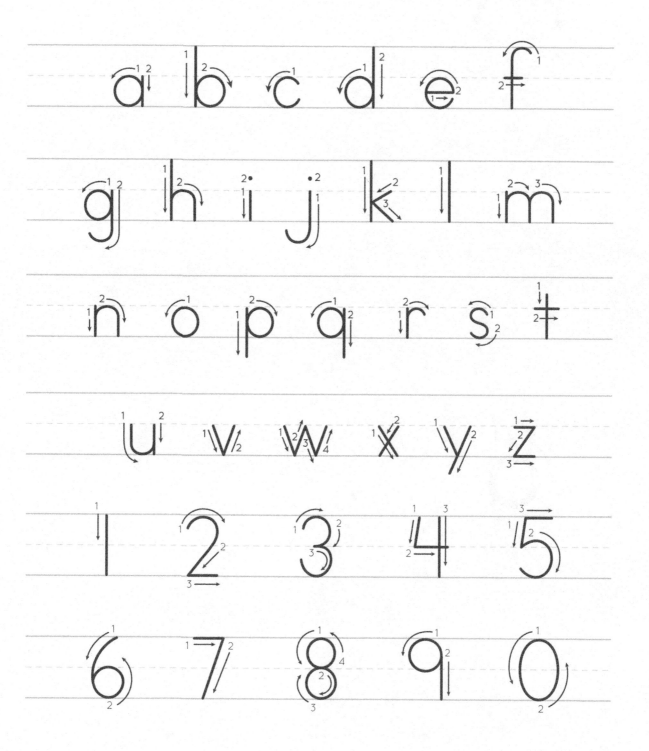

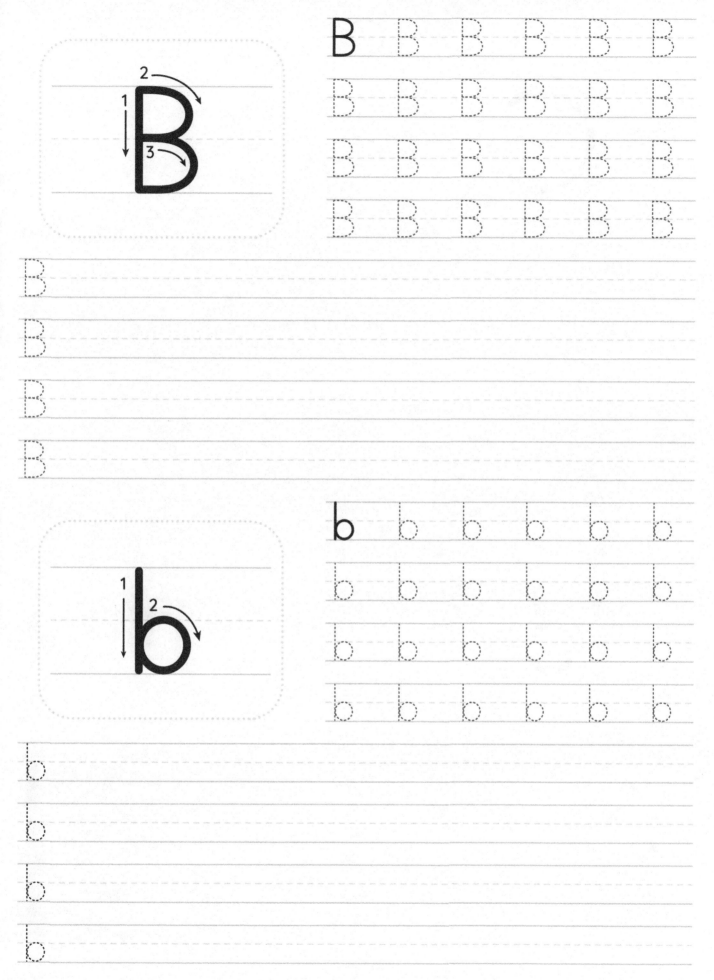

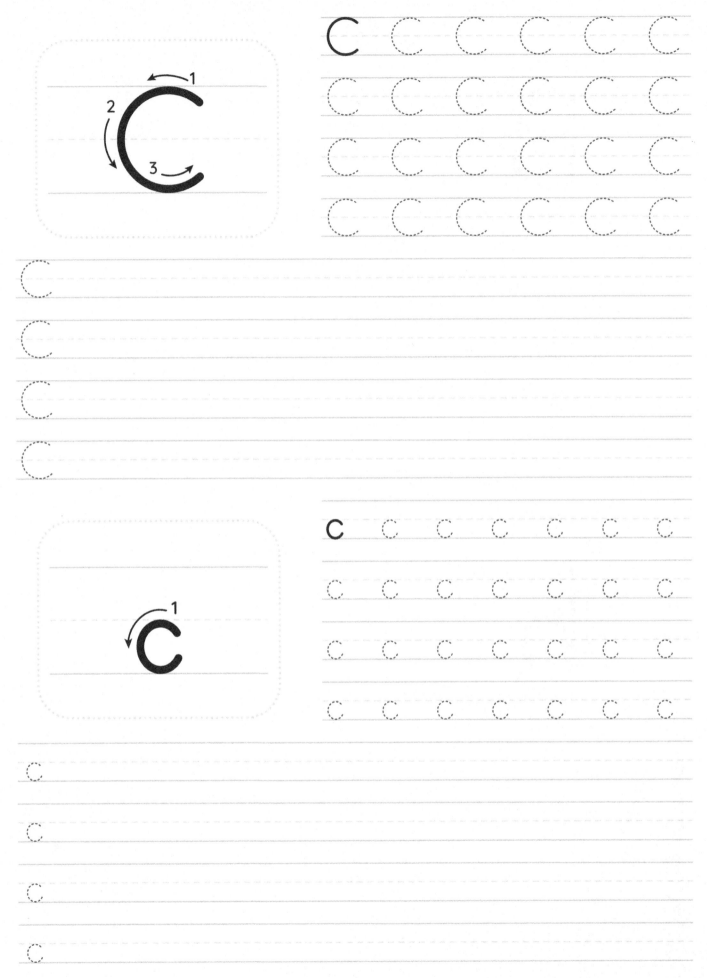

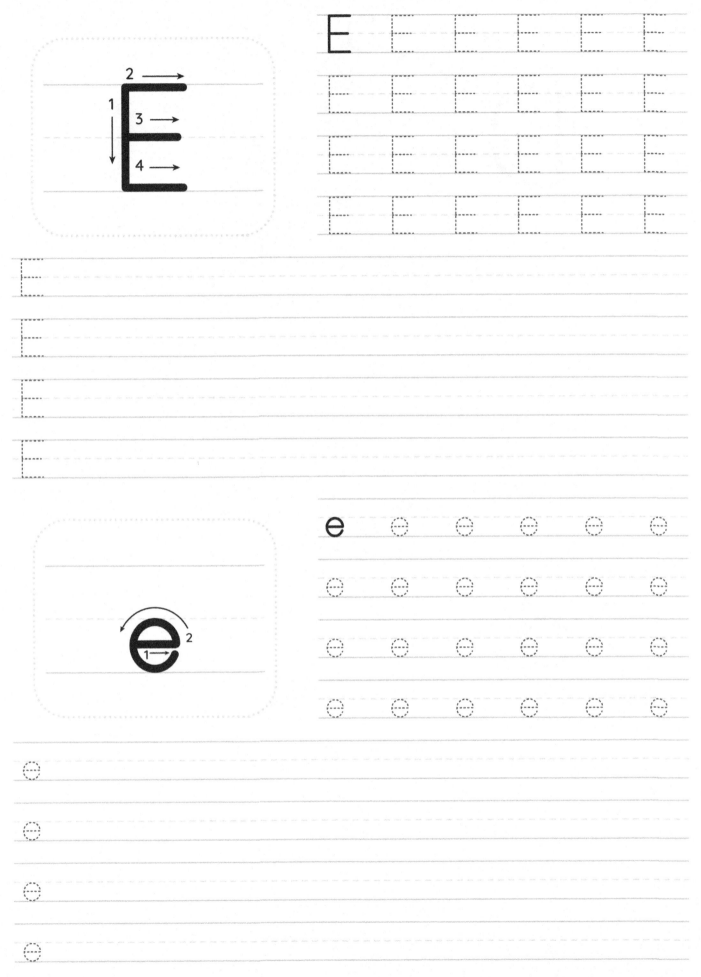

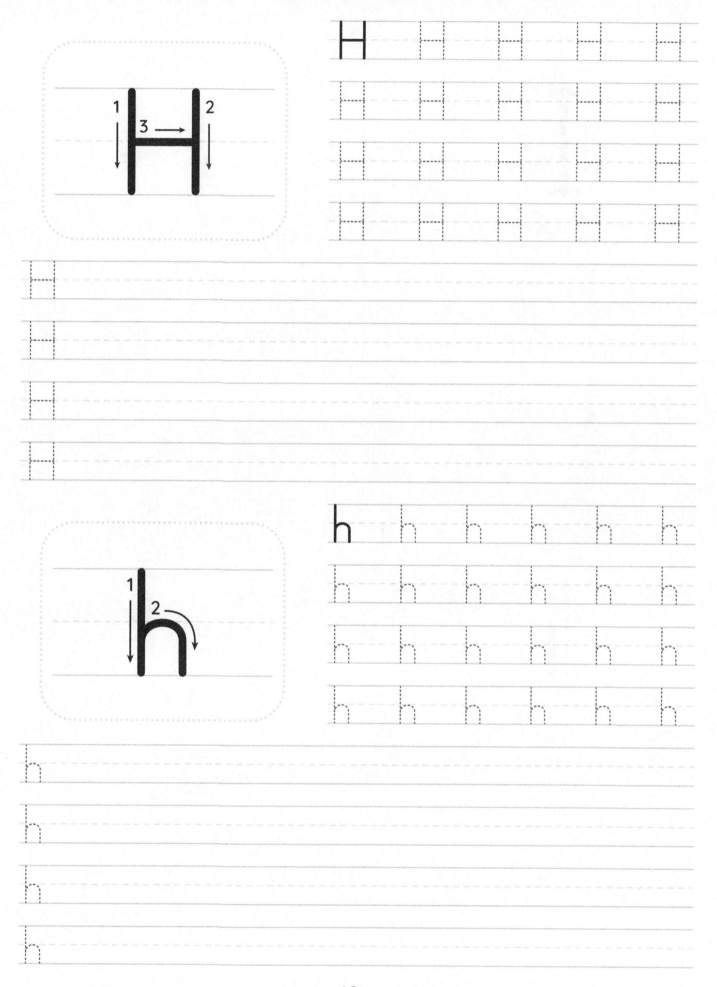

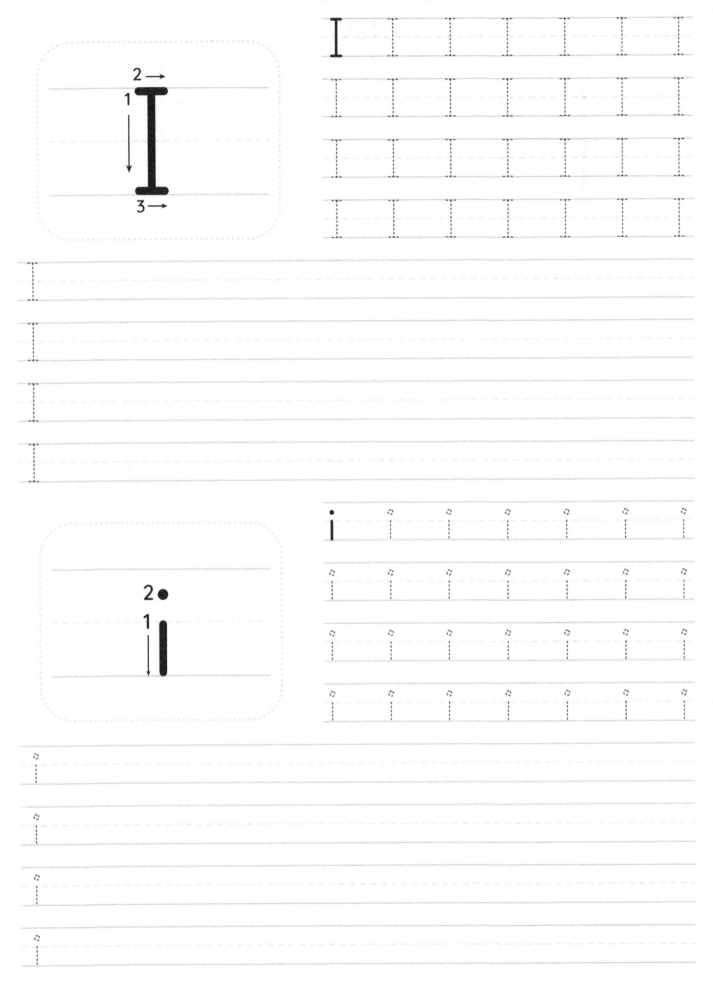

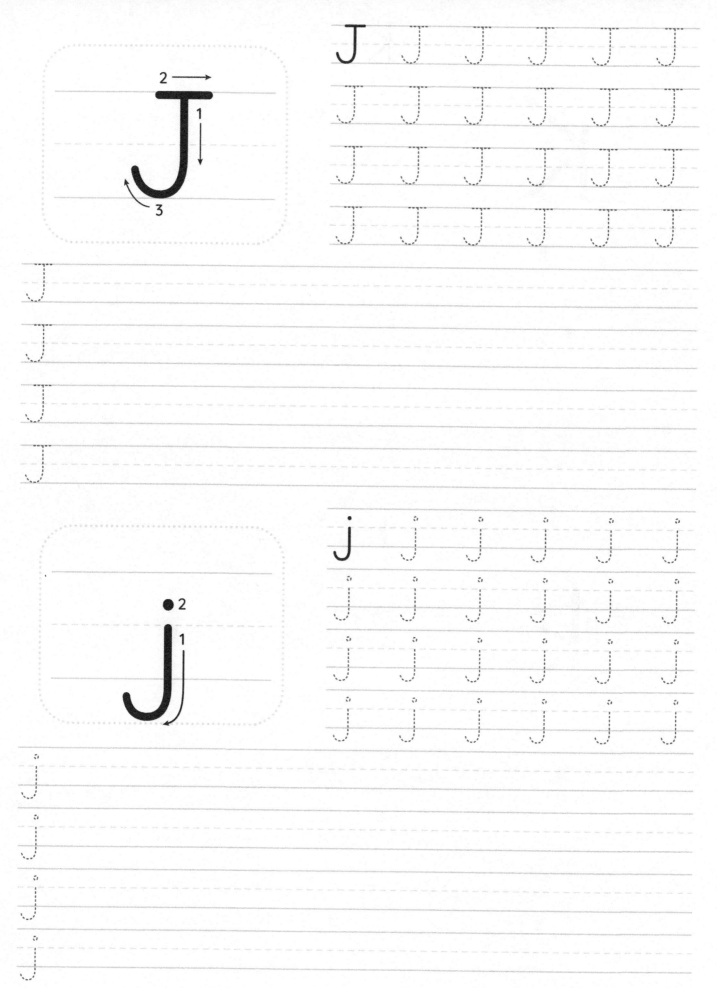

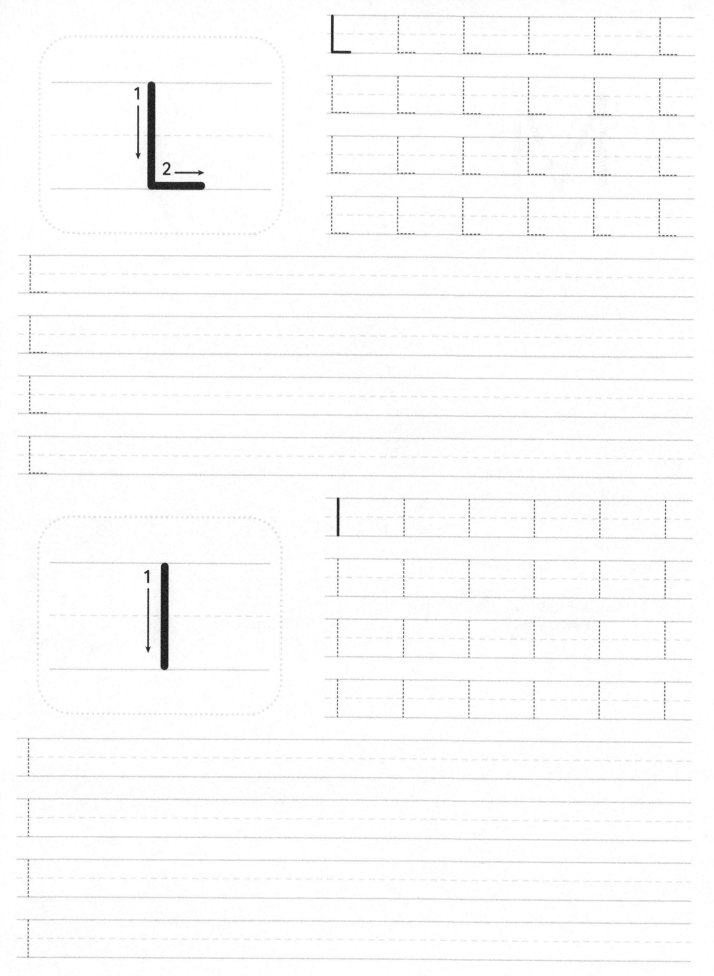

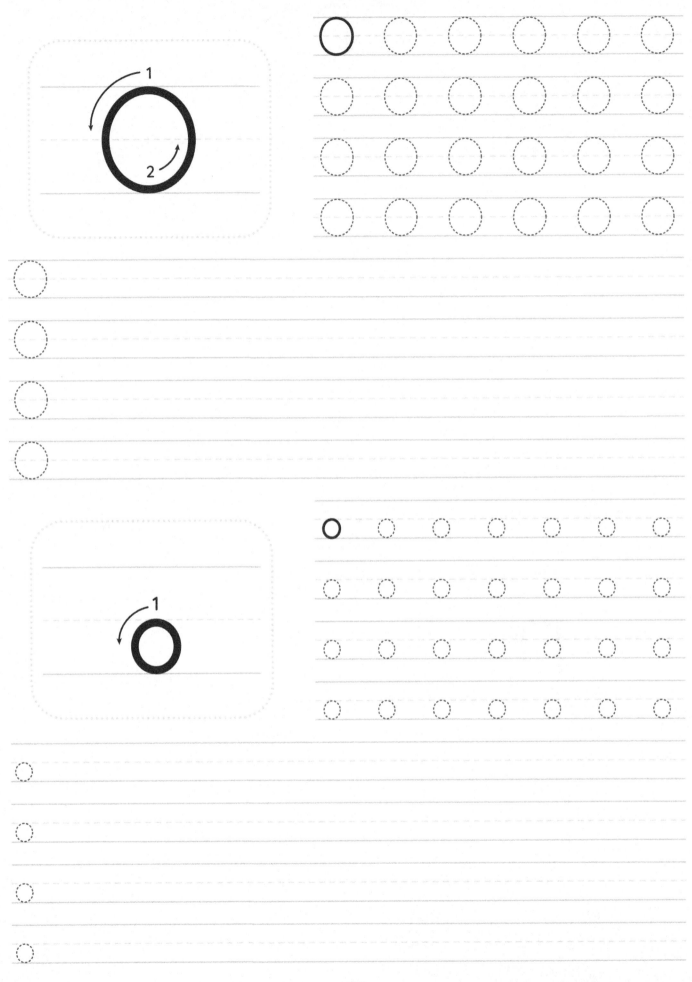

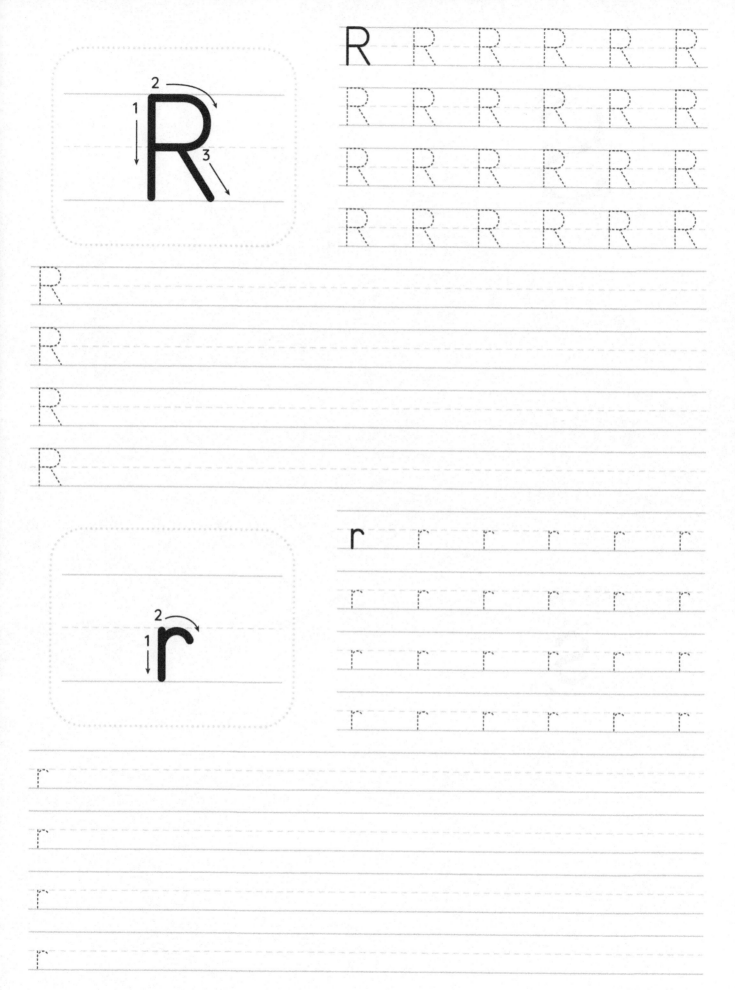

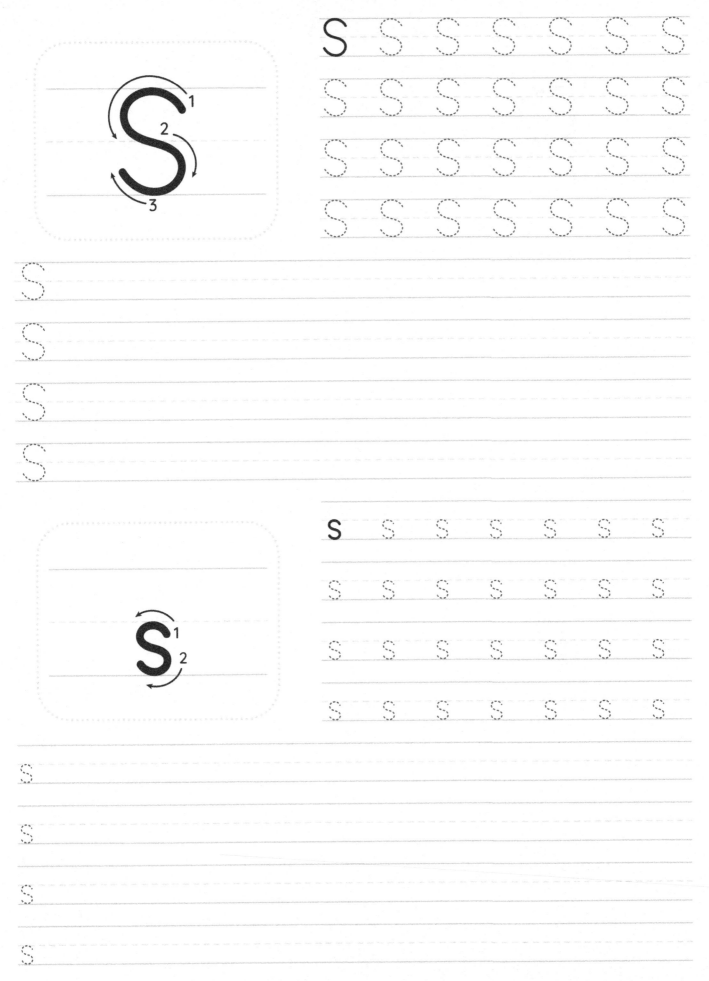

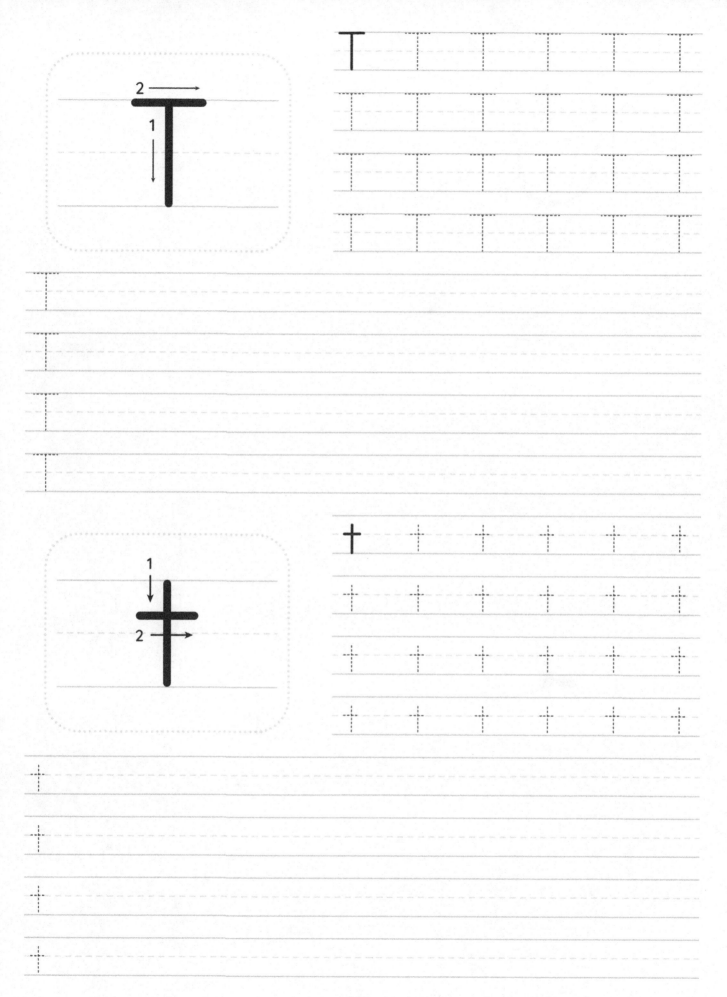

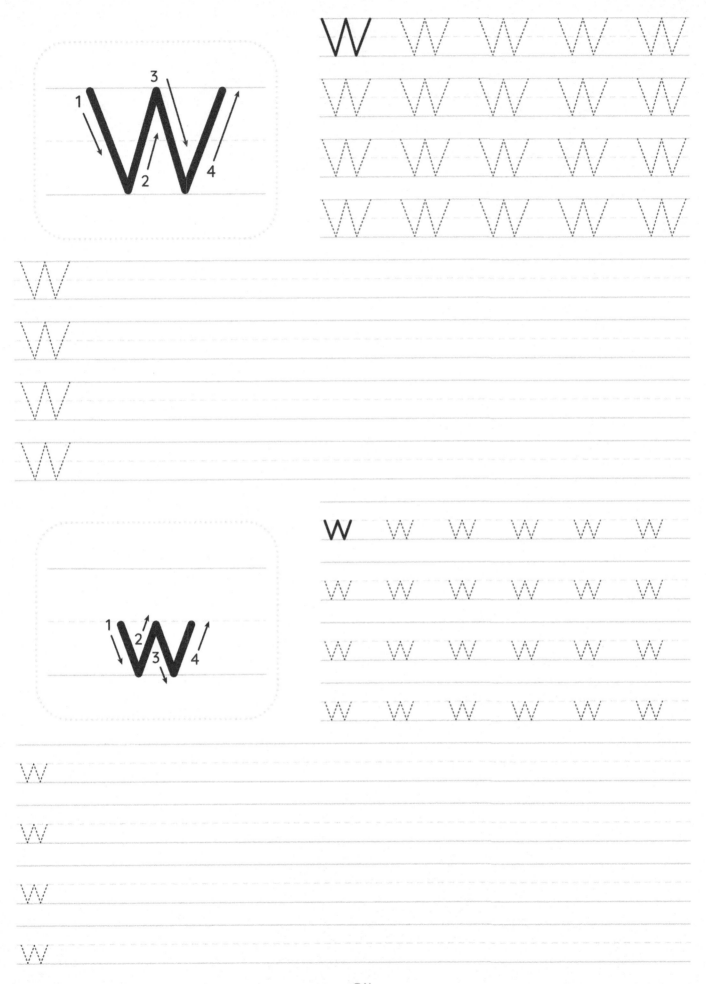

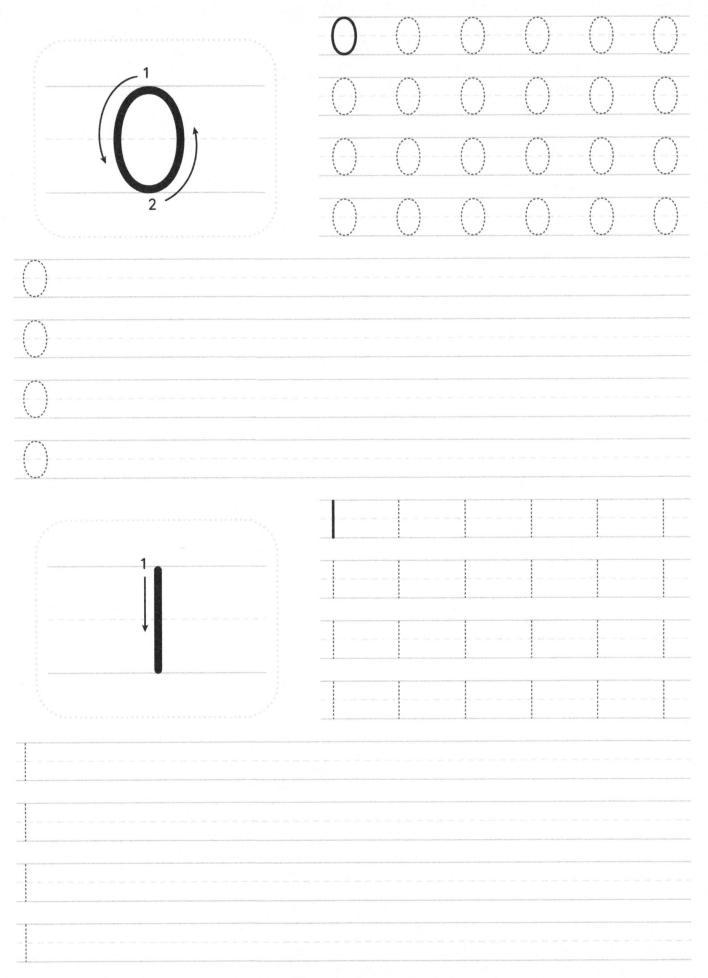

2 2 2 2 2 2
2 2 2 2 2 2
2 2 2 2 2 2
2 2 2 2 2 2

2
2
2
2

3 3 3 3 3 3
3 3 3 3 3 3
3 3 3 3 3 3
3 3 3 3 3 3

3
3
3
3

4

4   4   4   4   4   4

4   4   4   4   4   4

4   4   4   4   4   4

4   4   4   4   4   4

4

4

4

4

5   5   5   5   5   5

5   5   5   5   5   5

5   5   5   5   5   5

5   5   5   5   5   5

5

5

5

5

8

9

10 11 12 13 14 15 16 17 18 19 20 21 22

10 11 12 13 14 15 16 17 18 19 20 21 22

23 24 25 26 27 28 29 30 31 32 33

23 24 25 26 27 28 29 30 31 32 33

34 35 36 37 38 39 40 41 42 43 44

34 35 36 37 38 39 40 41 42 43 44

45 46 47 48 49 50 51 52 53 54 55

45 46 47 48 49 50 51 52 53 54 55

56 57 58 59 60 61 62 63 64 65 66

56 57 58 59 60 61 62 63 64 65 66

67 68 69 70 71 72 73 74 75 76 77 78

67 68 69 70 71 72 73 74 75 76 77 78

79 80 81 82 83 84 85 86 87 88 89

79 80 81 82 83 84 85 86 87 88 89

90 91 92 93 94 95 96 97 98 99 100

90 91 92 93 94 95 96 97 98 99 100

Elephant   Elephant   Elephant

Giraffe   Giraffe   Giraffe

Kangaroo   Kangaroo   Kangaroo

Dolphin   Dolphin   Dolphin   Dolphin

Penguin   Penguin   Penguin

Zebra   Zebra   Zebra   Zebra

Octopus   Octopus   Octopus

Flamingo   Flamingo   Flamingo

Apple   Apple   Apple

Banana   Banana   Banana

Cherry   Cherry   Cherry

Grape   Grape   Grape

Lemon   Lemon   Lemon

Orange   Orange   Orange

Strawberry   Strawberry

Watermelon   Watermelon

Carrot   Carrot   Carrot

Tomato   Tomato   Tomato

Lettuce   Lettuce   Lettuce

Broccoli   Broccoli   Broccoli

Cauliflower   Cauliflower

Pumpkin   Pumpkin   Pumpkin

Radish   Radish   Radish   Radish

Peas   Peas   Peas   Peas

Pizza   Pizza   Pizza   Pizza

Sandwich   Sandwich   Sandwich

Hamburger   Hamburger

Hotdog   Hotdog   Hotdog

Spaghetti   Spaghetti

Pancake   Pancake   Pancake

Waffle   Waffle   Waffle

Noodles   Noodles   Noodles

Sun   Sun   Sun   Sun

Moon   Moon   Moon   Moon

Mountain   Mountain   Mountain

Ocean   Ocean   Ocean   Ocean

Cloud   Cloud   Cloud   Cloud

Star   Star   Star   Star

Tree   Tree   Tree   Tree

Flower   Flower   Flower   Flower

Family   Family   Family

Mother   Mother   Mother

Father   Father   Father

Brother   Brother   Brother

Sister   Sister   Sister   Sister

Grandma   Grandma   Grandma

Grandpa   Grandpa   Grandpa

Home   Home   Home   Home

Believe Believe Believe Believe

Joyful Joyful Joyful Joyful

Happy Happy Happy Happy

Laugh Laugh Laugh Laugh

Brave Brave Brave Brave

Smile Smile Smile Smile

Hope Hope Hope Hope

Love Love Love Love

Kindness   Kindness   Kindness

Respect   Respect   Respect

Sharing   Sharing   Sharing

Honesty   Honesty   Honesty

Patience   Patience   Patience

Empathy   Empathy   Empathy

Forgive   Forgive   Forgive

Courage   Courage   Courage

Table   Table   Table   Table

Chair   Chair   Chair   Chair

Bookshelf   Bookshelf   Bookshelf

Television   Television   Television

Cup   Cup   Cup   Cup

Clock   Clock   Clock   Clock

Lamp   Lamp   Lamp   Lamp

Refrigerator   Refrigerator

Birthday   Birthday   Birthday

Halloween   Halloween

Thanksgiving   Thanksgiving

Christmas   Christmas

Easter   Easter   Easter   Easter

New Year   New Year   New Year

Valentine   Valentine   Valentine

Fourth of July   Fourth of July

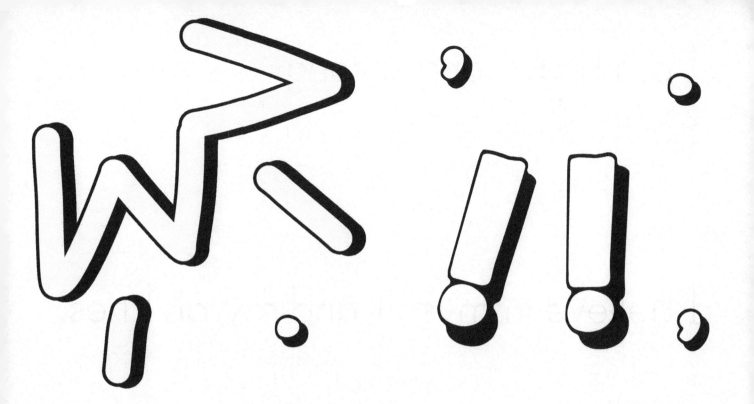

AFFIRMATIONS AND MOTIVATIONAL QUOTES

I am brave and strong

I am brave and strong

I am brave and strong

I believe in myself and my abilities

I believe in myself and my abilities

I believe in myself and my abilities

Mistakes help me learn and grow

Mistakes help me learn and grow

Mistakes help me learn and grow

I am unique and special

I am unique and special

I am unique and special

I am thankful for everything I have

I am thankful for everything I have

I am thankful for everything I have

I am kind and honest

I am kind and honest

I am kind and honest

I will be kind to myself and others

I will be kind to myself and others

I will be kind to myself and others

Differences make us special

Differences make us special

Differences make us special

I am worthy of happiness

I am worthy of happiness

I am worthy of happiness

Challenges make me stronger

Challenges make me stronger

Challenges make me stronger

I am loved and appreciated

I am loved and appreciated

I am loved and appreciated

I am proud of who I am

I am proud of who I am

I am proud of who I am

Everything will be okay

Everything will be okay

Everything will be okay

I am helpful and caring

I am helpful and caring

I am helpful and caring

I am a good person

I am a good person

I am a good person

Practice makes me perfect

Practice makes me perfect

Practice makes me perfect

I can learn new things every day

I can learn new things every day

I can learn new things every day

It's okay not to know everything

It's okay not to know everything

It's okay not to know everything

Learning is my superpower

Learning is my superpower

Learning is my superpower

I make others smile

I make others smile

I make others smile

Kindness is always a good choice

Kindness is always a good choice

Kindness is always a good choice

It's cool to be kind

It's cool to be kind

It's cool to be kind

Start the day with a smile

Start the day with a smile

Start the day with a smile

Enjoy the little things

Enjoy the little things

Enjoy the little things

Everything starts with a dream

Everything starts with a dream

Everything starts with a dream

Make your dreams happen

Make your dreams happen

Make your dreams happen

You become what you believe

You become what you believe

You become what you believe

You are loved more than you know

You are loved more than you know

You are loved more than you know

Always believe in yourself

Always believe in yourself

Always believe in yourself

If you can dream it, you can do it

If you can dream it, you can do it

If you can dream it, you can do it

Be kind, be brave, be you

Be kind, be brave, be you

Be kind, be brave, be you

You are stronger than you think

You are stronger than you think

You are stronger than you think

Every day is a new adventure

Every day is a new adventure

Every day is a new adventure

In every mistake, there is a lesson

In every mistake, there is a lesson

In every mistake, there is a lesson

Stay curious and keep exploring

Stay curious and keep exploring

Stay curious and keep exploring

Teamwork makes the dream work

Teamwork makes the dream work

Teamwork makes the dream work

Success begins with a single step

Success begins with a single step

Success begins with a single step

Do your best and forget the rest

Do your best and forget the rest

Do your best and forget the rest

Think positive, be positive

Think positive, be positive

Think positive, be positive

Never give up on your dreams

Never give up on your dreams

Never give up on your dreams

"What is a really sad strawberry called?" - A blueberry

"What has to be broken before you can use it?" - An egg

"What do you call a bear with no teeth?" - A gummy bear!

"Why does Peter Pan fly around so much?" - He 'Neverlands'

"Why don't oysters donate to charity?" - Because they're shellfish!

"How does a cow do math?"
- With a cow-culator!

"What's orange and sounds like a parrot?" - A carrot!

"What room can no one enter?"
- A mushroom

"Why was the math book sad?"
Because it had too many problems!

"What has keys but can never
unlock a door?" - A piano

"What has four wheels and flies?"
- A garbage truck

"Why is a baseball stadium
always cool?" - It is full of fans.

"What do you call a snowman in the summer?" - A puddle

"Where do cows go on Friday nights?" - They go to the moovies!

"What do you call a huge pile of cats?" - A meowntain!

"What can you catch but never throw?" - A cold!

"What do you call two bananas?"
- A pair of slippers!

"What is a robot's favorite snack?"
- Computer chips

"What animal is always at a
baseball game?" - A bat

"What do you call a dinosaur that
is sleeping?"- A dinosnore

"What goes up but never comes down?" - Your age

"What do frogs in Paris eat?" - French flies!

"What does a cow call an earthquake?" - A milkshake!

"Where do baby ghosts go during the day?" - Dayscare centers

"What falls but never gets hurt?"
- Snow

"What is blue but not heavy?"
- Light blue

"Can a kangaroo jump higher than
a house?" - Yes. Houses can't jump

"Which letter of the alphabet has
the most water?" - The "C"!

"What does a vegan zombie eat?"
- Graaains

"Who wears shoes while sleeping?"
- A horse

"What has a head and tail but
no body?" - A coin

"How do bees get to school?"
- A school buzz

"What is full of holes but still holds water?" - A sponge

"What has many rings but no fingers?" - A telephone

"What letter of the alphabet is a question?" - Y

"What has hands and a face, but no arms or legs?" - A clock

"What is yours but mostly used by others?" - Your name

"Which question can you never answer 'yes' to?" - Are you asleep?

"What flies all day but never goes anywhere?" - A flag

"What kind of lion never roars?" -- A dandelion

"What's black, white and blue?"
- A sad zebra

"I jump when I walk and sit when I stand. What am I?" - Kangaroo

"What's really easy to get into and hard to get out of?" - Trouble

"What begins with an E but only has one letter in it?" - An envelope

"What room do ghosts avoid?"
- The living room

"I sometimes run, but I cannot walk.
What am I?" - Your nose

"What has to be filled before you
can empty it?" - A cup

"What has a neck but no head?"
- A bottle

"What is always before you but can't be seen?" - The future

"What comes down but never goes up?" - Rain

"What can fill a room but take up no space?" - Light

"What begins with T, ends with T, and has T in it?" - A teapot

"I go up and down but never move. What am I?" - A staircase

"What lets you look right through a wall?" - A window

"What's black and white and read all over?" - A newspaper

"I am easy to lift but hard to throw. What am I?" - A feather

"Everyone has one, but no one can lose it. What is it?" - A shadow

"What will be yesterday but was tomorrow?" - Today

"What has many teeth, but cannot bite?" - A comb

"What is taken from you before you get it?" - Your picture

Lightning is five times hotter than the sun's surface.

A sneeze can travel at over 100 miles per hour.

A day on Venus is longer than a year on Venus.

Bananas are berries, but strawberries are not!

Honey never spoils if stored properly.
It can last thousands of years!

There are about 206 bones in an
adult human body.

The sun is a star over 1 million times
bigger than Earth!

The longest recorded flight of a
chicken is 13 seconds.

Cows have best friends and can get stressed when they are separated.

Space is completely silent. There's no air to carry sound.

There are more than 7,000 languages spoken around the world.

The electric eel can produce electric shocks of up to 600 volts.

The world's oldest known animal
lived to be 507 years old.

A honeybee can flap its wings 200
times per second.

Some bamboo species can grow up
to 35 inches in a single day.

Jellyfish are 95% water and have
no brain, blood, or heart.

Blue whales are the largest animals
ever to have lived on Earth.

Plants "talk" to each other using
chemical signals.

Some species of sea stars can
reproduce by splitting in half.

Water covers about 71% of
Earth's surface.

About seven octillion atoms
make up an adult human.

A typical cumulus cloud can weigh
more than a million pounds.

Rainbows can occur at night,
and they are called moonbows.

The human nose can remember
50,000 different scents.

There are more trees on Earth
than stars in the Milky Way.

The world's oldest known living tree
is over 4,800 years old.

Raindrops are not tear-shaped.
They are more like hamburger buns.

Owls can't move their eyes.
They have to turn their heads.

A woodpecker can peck 20 times per second.

The longest mountain range on Earth is mostly underwater.

Some species of turtles can breathe through their skin.

An adult human body has about 60,000 miles of blood vessels.

The Earth's magnetic field
protects us from solar radiation.

Seahorses are among the few
animals where males give birth.

Some fish can produce light
through bioluminescence.

The oldest known fossils are about
3.5 billion years old.

The longest word in the English
language has 45 letters.

The African mudfish can live
out of water for many months.

The Eiffel Tower can be 15 cm
taller in summer.

Mudskippers are fish that can climb,
walk, and jump on land.

Zebras are actually black with
white stripes.

A polar bear's fur is actually
transparent, not white.

A rainbow is actually a full circle,
but we can only see half of it.

The blue whale is the largest
animal ever known to have existed.

The speed of light is
299,792 kilometers per second.

A single oak tree can produce
10 million acorns over its lifetime.

Volcanic eruptions can create new
islands when they occur underwater.

Light from the Sun takes about
8 minutes to reach Earth.

Antarctica is the only continent without a native species of ants.

The only letter that doesn't appear in any U.S. state name is 'Q'.

More than 80% of the ocean is unexplored and unmapped.

Sound travels roughly four times faster in water than in air.

Water expands by about 9%
when it freezes into ice.

The human body is made up of
about 55-60% water.

A total solar eclipse occurs when
the moon completely covers the sun.

The planet Saturn has 146
confirmed moons in its orbit.

The Earth's core is primarily
composed of iron and nickel.

People can typically hear thunder
up to 15 miles away.

The moon has no atmosphere,
so it has no wind or weather.

The narwhal's "tusk" is actually
a long, spiral tooth.

Sharks have been around for over 400 million years, making them older than dinosaurs, trees, and even the rings of Saturn!

Saturn's rings are made of ice, rock, and dust particles. Some are as small as a grain of sand, while others are as big as houses!

Some species of fungi create 'zombies', infecting ants and taking control of their bodies to spread their spores.

The temperature in Antarctica can drop below -100°F (-73°C), making it the coldest place on Earth.

North American wood frogs can
freeze without dying. When they
thaw, their hearts start beating
again, and they come back to life!

Butterflies taste with their feet,
using special sensors to find out if
a plant is good for their caterpillars.

A giraffe's tongue is about 18 inches long and is dark blue to protect it from sunburn while eating from tall trees.

Jellyfish have been around for over 500 million years, making them one of the oldest living creatures on Earth.

A chameleon's tongue can be
as long as its body and can
shoot out at high speed to
catch insects.

Sea cucumbers can expel their
internal organs to deter predators
and then regenerate them
over time.

If you could invent a new ice cream flavor, what would it be? Describe its taste and ingredients.

Imagine you woke up with a superpower. What is it and how would you use it?

Write a letter to your future self. What advice would you give and what do you hope to accomplish?

Invent a new holiday. What is it called and how would people celebrate it?

If you could design a treehouse with any four rooms, what would they be?

An alien lands in your backyard and becomes your friend. What adventures do you have together?

Congratulations Handwriting Hero!

✦

You've made it to the end of this adventure in penmanship! You've practiced your letters, giggled at jokes, solved riddles, and even created your own stories. Your handwriting has improved, and your mind has grown.

Be proud of your progress.
Keep writing, keep learning, and keep being amazing!
Your next adventure awaits — pick up a pen and create your own story!
Great job, young writer. The world can't wait to read what you'll write next!

Made in the USA
Columbia, SC
22 October 2024

44828455R00063